Praise for

HEART OF HORSEMANSHIP©

Positive Impact Quotes:

I am in a state of awe, amazement, etc., and all positive from the equine therapy. It has shown me so much with words.

HOH has helped me see a greater need to bond with living creatures around me. – *AN*

I intentionally try to let go of all the dirt and garbage from my life and bring joy, peace, calmness in as I approach my horse. – *TG*

I always feel much more upbeat and helpful after each at the ranch. – *KT*

Because of connecting with my horse, I learned to focus and stay focused on the one task and clear my mind of all other things. – *CS*

I think the horses have been teaching me about communication, patience and calmness. – *SD*

Connection with Horses:

My connection with my horse is good so I can trust what we do. – *PD*

I felt "in the zone" with my horse a decent amount of my time with him. – *JL*

Being Present:

What I learn is that when I am with the horse, I am thinking about nothing else. What a great lesson to learn to be present with people and how complacent we become when we lose our fear. – *TO*

I finally feel connected with my horse when I "let go" and focus on her. – *PY*

I learned more about the idea of connection than I thought I would and about how much my mood could affect my horse. When I started getting frustrated or checked out, my horse would essential do the same thing. – *TA*

Bonding:

I find that the time I spend with my horse helps me to bond with people better. – *RT*

There were a few things I thought about today. It almost seems like I was able to start trusting the people in the group a little more by trusting and feeling safe and confident with my horse. – *JS*

Other testimonials:

I feel very enriched to have experienced not just this amazing program, but also these wholesome people. I am proud of what I have done to follow through with my commitment. I also feel that I have learned a valuable skill. I couldn't have picked a better location and memorable moments were had. I like how it was also ritualized almost spiritual. There were times when I didn't think about anything else. It woke me up, harnessed a beautiful energy zone. – *JL*

This experience has profoundly impacted my life and I will cherish this for years to come. Thank you for taking the time to invest in my recovery. I feel this has helped me grow as a person and has brought us together as a team. – *CH*

I feel much more present and could tell the difference in how the horse responded positively. – *SR*

I feel it would be better to be with Frosty then to be in heaven. Thank you for giving my life back. – *AH*

Ride It Out

Healing the Wounds of Warriors through the Energetic Connection with Horses

Ellen Kaye Gehrke, Ph.D.

Ride It Out: Healing the Wounds of Warriors
Through the Energetic Connection with Horses

Published by Rolling Horse Ranch
Copyright © 2019 by Ellen Kaye Gehrke, Ph.D.
All rights reserved.

Rolling Horse Ranch
Ramona, California
Email: ellen@rollinghorse.com

Publishing and editorial team: Author Bridge Media,
www.AuthorBridgeMedia.com
Project Manager and Editorial Director: Helen Chang
Editor: Jenny Shipley
Publishing Manager: Laurie Aranda
Cover Design: Deb Tremper
Cover photo credit: Dianna M. Webb

Library of Congress Number: 2019937172
ISBN: 978-1-7338336-0-8 – paperback
978-1-7338336-2-2 – ebook

Ordering Information:
Quantity sales. Special discounts are available on quantity purchases by
corporations, associations, and others. For details, contact the publisher
at the address above.

Printed in United States of America.

DEDICATION

This book is dedicated to all the men and women, active duty and veterans, who have taken the oath to protect and serve our country and its Constitution. They have willingly put their lives in harm's way so that we may enjoy the freedom and liberty we often take for granted in the United States of America. Many of these men and women have paid the ultimate price, and many are suffering the aftermath of fulfilling their duties.

This book is also dedicated to all the horses who have been partners in war and peace throughout mankind. By offering their hearts to our military for healing and support, they now take their rightful place beside our human war heroes.

CONTENTS

ACKNOWLEDGMENTS

This book would not have happened without the generosity and kind support from Danny Robinson of Blythe, California. He witnessed firsthand the transformation of the veterans who participated in the Heart of Horsemanship program and became one of its biggest cheerleaders.

Of course, the foundation for the work is due to the amazing partnership from the horses who have blessed my life and the lives of so many over the past twenty years: Franklin, Monte, Cougar, Shiloh, Rocket, Rusty, Tonopah, Tessie, Storm, Sassy, Maggie Mae, Reggie, and more. They have been my greatest teachers of loving kindness, awakeness, presence, resilience, patience, hope, and healing.

Many humans contributed to the evidence-based research that proves horses *do* help heal.

My research partner, Dr. Mike Myers, helped collect and analyze data in a way that was positive, noninvasive to the veterans, and inspiring. Other research partners—Kris Dores, Norm Dores, Dr. Paul Tontz, Dr. Ritika Bhawal, Dr. Peggy Ranke—created a dynamic and energetic team.

The initial research would not have moved forward without the cooperation of Veterans Village of San Diego under the leadership of Andre Simpson. Joe Costello, director of the Veterans Center in San Marcos, California, also supported the weekly trek of veterans to Rolling Horse Ranch as well as provided morning goodies to munch as we gathered together.

Thanks are also due to Dr. Gloria McNeal, the dean of the School of Health and Human Services at National University, San Diego, for providing motivation and time to champion the research with veterans and horses. Additional thanks go to Brian McCreery for special projects.

Tom Gunter, 101st Airborne Vietnam vet, is a champion of encouraging his fellow veterans toward the transformative healing that horses offer. And the brave men and women who have put their lives on the line and paid a huge price for our country deserve much credit for participating in the Heart of Horsemanship research the past few years: Richard True, Aaron Neely, Momma K, John Surmount, Becky, Jimmy, Joe, Dan, Brian, Jay, and Calvin, just to mention a few. They helped blaze a path for others to experience how horses provide a complementary approach to healing and reducing dependence on pharmaceuticals to relieve pain and suffering from anxiety, depression, and other PTSD-related symptoms.

I thank the team of counselors, wranglers, and experts at Rolling Horse Ranch: Ray Spence, Larry VanderPloeg, Trevor Osborne, K. L. Osborne, and Jennifer Lindsley. Gregary Marcum has also offered continuous cheering and help at the ranch. A special bow and memory to Clay and Mary Donohoe, of Nye, Montana who both mentored me for years. Clay gave me my first horse, Franklin, and modeled kindness and love for horses that only an ole cowboy could.

Thanks are also due to close friends Dr. Suzanne Evans, Dr. Karen Garman, Traci Steckler, and Sissy Helton and all the students, medical professionals, and corporate executives who, over the past fifteen years, came to the ranch and participated in our programs.

I want to thank my brothers, Bob, Mike, and Don, as well as my mother-in-law, Elfriede Gehrke, who prodded me to get this book done. Although he passed away in 2015, my dad, Dr. Samuel Kaye, is certainly smiling with pride. And deep in my soul, I owe my heart and my thanks to my deceased husband, Carsten P. Gehrke, who always provided the grounding for me to know this work had value. I think of him every day and am grateful for the twenty-one years we shared together. My cats, Kristina, Cali, and Cinch, and dogs, Bodhi and Gracie Joy, also deserve credit for their support, which came in the welcome form of nudges and licks.

Lastly, I thank the folks at Author Bridge Media who put the wind beneath my wings to make the book a reality. Thank you, Jenny Shipley, Laurie Aranda, Iris Sasing, and the rest of the team.

INTRODUCTION

Dark Moments

You are probably familiar with the list of symptoms for post-traumatic stress disorder, or PTSD.

Agitation.

Anxiety.

Emotional detachment.

Fear. Flashbacks.

Hostility, hypervigilance, irritability.

Insomnia, mistrust, nightmares.

Self-destructive behavior. Social isolation. Unwanted thoughts.

For veterans, these symptoms may be all too familiar. Counselors and other medical workers know that PTSD may not even be the only condition a person is suffering from. Many veterans do not receive the care or treatment they need. So, the symptoms start to feel like they're taking over their whole life.

Veterans are often overcome by unknown fears. Those who suffer from PTSD are often afraid to go outside, afraid to be around people, afraid they won't be seen as *themselves* anymore, even after everything they have experienced and all that they have given our country.

It's hard for them to talk about their feelings. If they do, it's most likely with someone who has been in the military—someone who has had a similar experience.

One veteran in our program, a retired Navy SEAL, says that having PTSD feels like carrying around a rucksack that's loaded up with troubles, heavier than rocks.

A Vietnam vet remembers being spit on and called a "baby killer" when he returned from the war. He held that inside for fifty years, broken, because he had to figure out how to just get through life. He existed and got by and raised a family, but he never addressed that part of his past. And now that he's retired, those experiences have come back to haunt him.

Another veteran revealed that she was on the brink of committing suicide. She slept with a gun in her mouth every single night for a year. Every night she was in so much pain that she asked herself, Is tonight the night I'm going to pull the trigger?

She had lost all hope.

No matter what branch of the service they were in, or when they served, many veterans are left feeling the same way. In their darkest moments, they wonder, Can this ever change? Can I ever feel better?

Is there any hope?

A Ray of Hope

It doesn't have to be this way.

Whether you are a veteran yourself, a counselor or health-care worker, or anyone who works with veterans, it is important you know that evidence-based treatment options exist to help those living with PTSD. They can pick up the pieces and find peace. They can feel safe, supported, and openhearted. And they can do it by learning to be in partnership with another sentient being: horses.

The **HEART OF HORSEMANSHIP**© program, which I created with colleagues in 2015, is one such option.

This program works in partnership with horses to transform the lives of veterans living with PTSD. More than five hundred thousand combat veterans from the Vietnam, Iraq, and Afghanistan wars have been diagnosed with PTSD and traumatic brain injury (TBI). Horsemanship programs throughout the country offer an alternative, nonpharmaceutical approach that helps these veterans feel more connected with themselves and those around them.

These programs take veterans through a journey to unlock their hearts. By creating and building on a connection from the heart, those who suffer from PTSD can become calmer, less anxious, and more grounded.

One **HEART OF HORSEMANSHIP**© participant described what our program did for him:

"It feels like you've been holding your breath for a long time, and then you finally get to exhale. You feel a sense of relief. You can take off that hundred-pound rucksack and lay down that burden you've been carrying around for too long."

Another said,

"I think I've come home."

And the Vietnam vet who remembered being spit on?

He was able to process his experiences and even share them with his wife and children. The woman on the brink of suicide? She gradually felt safe enough to put down the gun. She realized she could be a whole person—and by the end of the program, her beautiful laughter uplifted us all.

That connection is possible for all people who are around horses.

When you are with a horse, you will see that a sentient being cares about you, and that it's okay to care for the horse too. You will know that someone has your back, without judgment. You can rely on your horse and know that, just by being around it and letting yourself go through a softening process, your horse is going to help you.

Initially, it may sound scary—the veterans didn't really

know what they were walking into or what they were going to get—but in creating a connection from their hearts, the veterans began to unravel the turmoil inside and open up safely.

Horses gently chisel the armor around a warrior's heart until that person realizes he or she does not need to wear the armor anymore.

Most importantly, these veterans felt hope again. They learned they *can* find help. They discovered that they *can* get through this. They don't have to be isolated—and they found a connection back to life.

These veterans made enormous sacrifices and showed great courage to defend the values and people of the USA. They deserve to be served by us, and to feel whole and alive again.

HEART OF HORSEMANSHIP©

Although I've loved horses all my life, I didn't start to work with them until I was an adult. I didn't even get my first horse until I was forty-three years old. And it wasn't until then that I started to really understand what horses were all about.

That was the beginning of the years-long journey during which I explored and researched this question: How do you make a connection with a horse?

As I adopted, gentled, and learned to train horses, I

learned how to show up for the horse, how to communicate, and how by being with a horse can make people feel good. I earned certificates in equine-guided education and equine-facilitated learning. I brought horses to clinic after clinic. And I dove right in to conducting horse-centered workshops and training for business, organizational management, education, health care, and more.

As a full-time professor, I wanted to focus on research and education. I really did not have an interest in becoming a therapeutic riding center. I wanted to provide a unique way to help others be mindful and touch their authentic selves in the presence of horses.

In 2005, I started doing research about the human-animal bond and the impact horses can have on people. I've since published articles in *The International Journal for Human Caring*; *JOJ Nursing & Health Care*; *Journal of Military, Veteran and Family Health*; *The Journal of Research in Innovative Teaching*; *Professional Association of Therapeutic Horsemanship International Strides*; *Journal of Alternative and Complementary Medicine*; and the *Journal of Equine Veterinary Science*.

I've led workshops, programs, and seminars with hundreds of people. And all of them have been touched by the heart connection they made with the horses. I knew horses made a difference, but I couldn't find much evidence-based research about that impact.

In February 2015, several colleagues and I started a

pilot program we called the **HEART OF HORSEMANSHIP**© with a group of combat veterans living at a residential treatment center in San Diego, California. The cowboys and wranglers who work in the program have been in the service. I'm not a veteran myself, but I did spend seven years teaching on military bases. I have the utmost respect for the military, and the issues with PTSD they experience concerned me. Creating a program to help veterans heal from those symptoms through a heart-to-heart connection with a horse allows me to honor their service and give back.

Danny, one of the founders of the program (and an Air Force veteran), likes to say, "Ellen and her cowboys are a special breed." And it's true. No one else has the same approach we do.

In building the **HEART OF HORSEMANSHIP**© program, I looked at other programs to see if I could find anything that reflected our approach. One of the things I noticed was that most therapeutic riding programs were missing the emphasis on the connection from the heart. Many focus primarily on teaching skills around horses. The heart connection was a secondary outcome.

We moved that connection to the forefront and designed the research to determine if the physiology of the horse and human could be connected by measuring heart-rate variability. We wanted to provide evidence-based research to validate that working with horses can help heal the wounds of combat, and we wanted to offer a nonpharmaceutical approach to the healing process. We created a safe place for veterans to express themselves and transcend the trauma they've been carrying around.

This book is offered as a way to share what happened to those veterans who worked with horses in a heart-based way. It tells the story of how the veterans found their way back to wholeness in their lives.

Let's Make a Real Connection

Reading this book may be like starting a relationship.

My advice to you—in reading and in love—is to stay open and allow for what unfolds. Do the dance. Enjoy the journey of sharing life with those who made an authentic connection with another being and felt their heart grow bigger and stronger as a result.

If you are a veteran reading this book, please know that this type of heart-centered equine program exists; you can ask your counselor at the VA or Veteran's Center to help you find one. If you are a case manager, counselor, or health-care professional working with veterans, you will see how beneficial a program like this can be. If you are a spouse or family member, encourage your loved one to seek help, and join in if possible. My team and I provide evidence that shows how this is a valid and reliable way to minimize symptoms associated with PTSD. If you have a riding facility, you may be seeking ways to serve your clients with an approach that is meaningful and sustainable. Repositioning your program to add a treatment option like this is one way to provide that.

And if you fit into none of these categories, or more than one, this book will show you an evidence-based approach to treating the very serious issues around PTSD that exist in our society.

Each chapter revolves around a theme that contributes to reducing PTSD symptoms and building meaningful relationships. The chapters follow the progression of meeting and making a connection, to realizing the energetic dynamics of relationships, to launching a more fulfilling life.

By the end of the book, I want veterans (and their families) to realize they do not have to endure loss and isolation, suffering the pain that comes from trauma. Instead, I want them to feel *hope*, just like at the beginning of a new relationship.

The Gift of Hope

You will witness the veterans in this book connect back with themselves and discover their innate gifts: the gifts of connection, of presence, of becoming open. As you do, you may want to explore this type of healing and the gift of hope that many have lived without for so long.

I hope you will realize that equine therapy is an

evidence-based method of addressing trauma-related healing—an alternative or complementary approach to traditional treatment that is not drug related. This method of equine-partnered therapy has been shown to reduce suffering and help veterans regain their confidence, connection, and motivation to live. Veterans have stated that in the program they discover a similar type of brotherhood and sisterhood they often felt in the military. Our intention is to create a desire for you to feel safe to try this method of healing.

Working with horses has a deep element of connecting to nature. Biologist and Pulitzer Prize–winning author E. O. Wilson and others have confirmed that humans have a deep need to feel connected to nature and the universal field of life. With this experience comes a sense of peace and wholeness that I hope you get to embrace.

Chapter 1

ORIENTATION

Cowboys Don't Walk

I used to visit a horse ranch in Montana owned by Mary and Clay Donohoe, who were like parents to me. In fact, Clay gave me Franklin, my first horse, in 1987.

During that visit, we were sitting around the breakfast table one morning when Clay told me that a pack string had broken loose. "I think one of the horses is up on the flat," he said. "Probably somebody had better go and find it."

Apparently that somebody would be me!

So Clay took me along—still wearing my shorts and running shoes—to track the horse in the mountains. When we drove up as close as we could in the truck, he said, "Why don't you go on up that mountain and see if you can find it?" When I asked why he wasn't going with me, he replied, "I'm wearing cowboy boots. Cowboys don't walk. We *ride*."

At that time, I didn't even know how to put a halter on

a horse, but I took the halter and a bucket of oats and hiked to the top of the mountain. Just as I walked up the side, I saw the horse grazing. How the heck did Clay know this horse was here? I wondered.

I looked at the horse—a beautiful buckskin—and he looked back at me. My heart skipped a beat. He blinked and went back to eating. I walked closer, my heart pounding harder with every step. I thought he would just run off, but he let me come up and pet him. I felt such peace as soon as I touched him. He nuzzled me for a second and then plowed his muzzle into the bucket of oats I had brought to bribe him. While he was busy, I figured out how to put the halter on.

"Do you want to walk down the mountain with me?" I asked him. And he just came along! I couldn't believe it.

When we got down the mountain, Clay was snoozing in the pickup with a country-western radio station playing. He sat up when he heard me, and then he just stared for a moment. "Well, I'll be!" he said. "You actually found the horse!"

Something happened that day. I felt something soften in my heart, right when I met this horse. That was the first time I realized I could have that heart connection and how strong it could be with an animal that isn't a human.

I felt like I had come home in some sort of knowing way. I felt like I had found a partner.

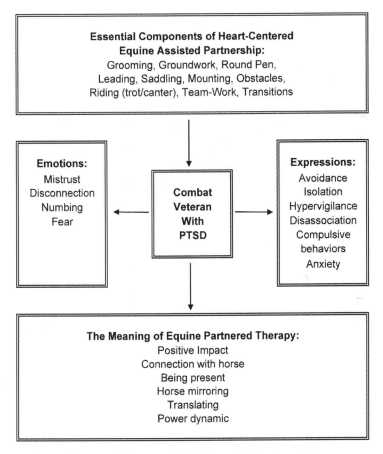

Essential Components of Heart-Centered Equine Assisted Partnership:
Grooming, Groundwork, Round Pen, Leading, Saddling, Mounting, Obstacles, Riding (trot/canter), Team-Work, Transitions

Emotions:
Mistrust
Disconnection
Numbing
Fear

Combat Veteran With PTSD

Expressions:
Avoidance
Isolation
Hypervigilance
Disassociation
Compulsive behaviors
Anxiety

The Meaning of Equine Partnered Therapy:
Positive Impact
Connection with horse
Being present
Horse mirroring
Translating
Power dynamic

Roadmap to Treating PTSD with Equine Therapy

Why Horses?

Horses and other domesticated animals have evolved in tandem with the needs of humans. Throughout history, horses were thought of as tools or instruments: something to use to make work easier, whether plowing fields or pulling milk wagons and fire engines. For much of history, militaries fought wars on horseback, turning those horses into soldiers as well.

Gradually, horses have transitioned from beasts of burden into subjects of pleasure—from race horses to dressage and show horses—and ultimately into partners. Cowboys understood the importance of their relationships with their horses. And that evolution into partnership—in healing and health care and as a support system—is still happening.

Humans experience biophilia, which is an innate need to connect with nature. Horses offer a bridge to that connection. A lot of the social dynamics of horses relate to humans as well. Horses live in herds similar to how people live in communities. And they have very clear hierarchies. I have eight horses, and you can tell very clearly who is number one and who is number eight. The number one has to earn respect, not by being the biggest bully, but by being the leader that takes care of the herd.

Horses are prey animals, so their natural state is to be fearful. We have this joke that horses are afraid of only two things: things that move and things that don't move.

Ultimately, we build a relationship with the horse so it trusts us not to take it into an unsafe place. But that fear is still there, underneath the surface.

That predator-prey relationship makes sense to veterans. It reminds them of being the hunter or the hunted in terms of war and combat. Combat veterans, in particular, have a heightened sense of vigilance.

It is this understanding and the ability to relate to that feeling of fear and vigilance that allow horses to be such effective partners in therapy for veterans.

Horse-Partnered Therapy

Many types of therapies exist. A person might take yoga, float in a water tank, or do expressive arts. It can be a thrill for someone to catch a great wave on a surfboard, ride a motorcycle through the mountains, or hike in a forest. But a person engages in all of these modalities alone.

Equine-partnered therapy is one of the only modalities for veterans that encourages making a heart connection with another sentient being. This is done in a safe place, which also allows veterans to see how that connection feels in their bodies.

When you are in a relationship with a horse, you have a safe partner who doesn't care if you have a brain injury, if you're two feet tall, or if you are purple! You don't have to worry about being judged or criticized. All your horse

Overview of 8-week curriculum

Week	Goal/Intention	Target PTSD Symptom	Group Activities
1	Establishing/building trust	Lack of Trust/Isolation	Meeting/Grooming, "Mutual Choosing", Learning horse language
2	Building Connection/Presence	Anxiety	Grooming, Groundwork/Round Pen/Lock-on
3	Sustaining Connection/Awareness	Relationship Issues	Grooming, Groundwork/Round Pen/leading Activity
4	Working Together/Flow	Anxiety	Grooming, Groundwork/Round Pen, Leading, Saddling Preparation
5	Opening Heart/Managing Fear	Disassociation	Grooming, Groundwork, Round Pen, Leading, Saddling, Mounting, Riding (walk)
6	Energetic Heart Synergistics	Irritability	Grooming, Groundwork, Round Pen, Leading, Saddling, Mounting, Riding (walk), Obstacles
7	Somatically Enhancing Mindfulness/Performance	Negative Beliefs and Detachment	Grooming, Groundwork, Round Pen, Leading, Saddling, Mounting, Obstacles, Riding (trot/canter)
8	Recognizing Wholeheartedness/ Mind, Body, Spirit	Hypervigilance and Social Isolation	Grooming, Groundwork, Round Pen, Leading, Saddling, Mounting, Obstacles, Riding (trot/canter), Team-Work, Transitions

cares about is that you're present and that you show up with your heart. They will be responsive to you if you show up for them.

Energetically, horses are also very sensitive. A horse's heart is five times the size of a human's, which increases the size of what is called the bioenergetic field around it. Research has shown that the heart has an energy field around it that touches others in their fields. That big heart field has been shown to influence the openness and vulnerability of humans.

Horses don't have a well-developed frontal cortex, so they are designed to respond to what is happening now, not the past or the future. It's not fair to say they don't have a memory, because if you haven't seen a horse in a while, it will be very happy to see you. They remember or have physical experiences of things that have happened to them. But they are nonjudgmental. They don't hold grudges. They want to be in relationship, and that lends itself very nicely to being able to help people who may have issues in that area.

Part of the healing in veterans' lives comes from learning to build a relationship with a horse.

Heart Rate Variability (HRV)

One thing that sets our program apart is the research we did with the participants.

In 2005, at a Heart Math workshop, I came to understand the importance of heart-rate variability, or HRV, in the autonomic nervous system. Heart-rate variability measures the beat-to-beat changes in the heart. The more variance there is, the better the heart rate. People tend to get this confused, because they think your heartbeat should be a nice, even beat. But the reality is that if your heartbeat is even, meaning your heart-rate variability is low, you're not very healthy.

When we first started the **HEART OF HORSEMANSHIP**© program with veterans, we wanted to see if they had physiological changes when interacting with horses. No other research existed to determine this. So we measured the veterans' heart-rate variability before seeing the horses (using a non-invasive HRV camera, which gives readings in one minute with 94 percent accuracy) and again after working with them for a few hours.

We weren't sure what was going to happen, but the results were remarkable.

Every week, starting the very first week, the veterans' heart-rate variability improved from the moment they showed up to the moment they left. What's more, their starting points—the measurements taken at the beginning of each session—started at a lower and lower baseline. The readings postsession were phenomenal, reflecting the level of balance one would expect to see in the autonomic nervous system of trained athletes. Measurements improved from the beginning of a session to the end of that same session, as well as from week to week.

We saw a significant balance of the autonomic nervous system of veterans who were around horses, and that's why we jokingly began calling the work "horse pills." The more doses taken—the more time spent with horses—the better!

PANAS

The other task veterans were asked to fill out was a self-reported survey before and after each session. We deliberately decided against using any PTSD-measurement instruments because the veterans claimed that filling them out often triggered their PTSD.

Instead we used the Positive-and - Negative Affect Survey (PANAS) to measure how participants felt (happy, irritated, joyful, etc.) at the start of the session and how those feelings changed by the end of the session with the horses.

What's interesting is that even though the veterans, in every single cohort, showed physiological improvement on the very first day, their self-reports typically didn't reflect the improvement until the fourth week. This showed that the veterans didn't think they felt much different—but they were changing all along.

After talking to their partners, counselors, and other people in their lives, we discovered that the veterans were perceived by others as calmer. They were more relaxed, right from the very first week. Their therapists and case-workers told us that the biggest thing they noticed was the reduction in anxiety, which was also scientifically shown as significant in the veterans' PANAS results. When people aren't as anxious, they are able to make better decisions and own up to some of their other issues.

The **HEART OF HORSEMANSHIP**© participants experienced a newfound sense of connection to themselves and others. They gained a more realistic perspective on their PTSD. And, in partnership with horses, these veterans were able to engage in a healing journey. Through the evidence-based research conducted in tandem with the work, that journey has proven to have profound and significant results.

A Journey to Wholeness

Each chapter in this book is based on one session of the **HEART OF HORSEMANSHIP**© program.

Each session builds on the ones before it, building horsemanship skills and working to reduce two of the worst aspects of PTSD: anxiety and depression. Each chapter also works to rebuild the connection to the world through a continuing awareness of one's physical, energetic, and intentional presence.

Reestablishing a Feeling of Trust. In the first session, the veterans meet the horses who will become their partners on their journey of transformation. Horses are authentic, safe beings who open their hearts to the veterans, which allows the veterans to tap into their authentic self. That is the beginning of trust.

Recognizing and Building a Connection. As they get to know their horses, the veterans begin to meet their true self. They realize they can care for—and understand—another being. The silent language of behavior leads to a new connection, which is also the connection back to their own hearts.

Sustaining a Connection through Staying Present. It feels wonderful for the veterans to discover that new connection with their horse partner, but it is so easy to get distracted. If their mind wanders while working with their horse, they lose the connection. When they recognize the connection and stay present, a relationship builds.

Going Together. By session four, the veterans learn to relax their bodies and "go" with the horses, and then the horses will go with them. This is often described as "flow." Going together builds softness and allows a give-and-take to develop that opens the heart in true connection.

Communicating with Confidence. The veterans also learn they have to be the leader, not by dominating but by partnering, and taking the leader role helps the participant build confidence. The veterans lead with an open heart to get a better response from their horse partner and to create more joy in themselves and their accomplishments.

Finding Aliveness in Your Body. In this chapter, we examine how the veterans open up to more awareness of sensations and learn to handle emotional surges in a way that serves them. They discover how regulating the energy in their body can be used in relationship with their horse. This self-regulation can also be very helpful in modulating the upheavals that can occur with PTSD.

Working Together in Confident Performance. By this point, the horse and the veteran realize they have a job to do: form a relationship and together accomplish tasks on an obstacle course mindfully, with their hearts and from their connection. This chapter seeks to remove any remaining fears and replace them with confidence and awareness—of the veterans themselves, their horse, and others.

Feeling Wholehearted. At this final stage of the program, the veterans have discovered a flow of things that go right without having to think about them—what is often labeled "unconscious competence." We reflect on the veterans' journey and celebrate how far they have traveled during the eight-week program.

At the end of this journey, the veterans become not only better riders and horsemen, but also better connected to the world around them. They enjoy the time with their horse and their friends, and their hearts start to feel whole again.

The veterans realize that if they can do this, they can do other things out in the world.

Last day of Cohort Four- Veterans, Wranglers, Counselors, Research Team

Chapter 2

REESTABLISHING A
FEELING OF TRUST

Ellen and Storm

Storm is a horse who came to live on Ellen's ranch in 2003, when he was seven years old. I was practicing obstacles with Storm one day, and I really wanted him to walk across a tarp, but he was scared.

I kept trying to get him to walk over the tarp, but he continued to freak out and back away. He whinnied loudly and got upset if he did go across, his feet prancing all over the place. The trainer I was working with told me, "You may have gotten him across the tarp, but he still doesn't feel very good inside about it. You're going to have to set up a situation for that horse to feel good about himself and his relationship with you."

That's when I realized that I needed to find a "try"—a time when Storm was trying to do what I asked—and reward the try. Then I could keep building on that small success.

It took me a long time with Storm, but I recognized that he was scared, so I rewarded him every time he made any little bit of effort. Eventually, I think he realized I wasn't going to take him someplace knowingly dangerous. So he tried to do what I asked because he began to trust me. And when he finally walked across the tarp, he looked at me like, What's the big deal?

A Feeling of Trust

Storm taught me an important lesson (other than just how stubborn a horse can be!). I learned that if you force somebody to do something, it doesn't stick. But if you make people feel okay about who they are inside, they might try some different things.

Before doing any work with another being, we need to create an environment of safety and trust.

Horses are always assessing who is safe enough to trust and lead the herd. They are looking for a place to feel safe. And when they feel safe, when they can be vulnerable, they can trust this relationship. That is true for the veterans as well. When we set them up in a way that is safe for them to keep trying, they get rewarded. They start to trust.

If we didn't spend time building this feeling of trust,

the relationship that builds—if it's built at all—is accidental. It's not conscious. If we didn't do these trust-building activities, the program would probably look the same, but it wouldn't feel the same, and it wouldn't lead to these same results.

With the **HEART OF HORSEMANSHIP**© program, the consciousness that is brought to each relationship is what opens up people's hearts.

The heart is critical in how we live and who we are. We find that by approaching a relationship from the heart in a mindful, conscious, open way, the veteran can start to change inside. This relationship doesn't just have to be with a horse. Once they understand and anchor that sensation and behavior, veterans can take that experience and create it with their significant other, children, friends, and family. Veterans often describe feeling anxious around people or withdrawing from them, even the people who love and support them. Building trust allows those relationships to be rebuilt and become stronger. From there, the veterans keep building connections outward, into their communities and other relationships.

To build trust, we start with the same rituals every session. Then, to help the veterans become aware of their energy, we introduce them to the horses, and we start building that relationship at the first moment of connection.

Our Regular Rituals

Each session of the **HEART OF HORSEMANSHIP**© begins the same way: with certain rituals that create connection, continuity, and trust. The rituals also relate to the veterans' military experience with symbols and behaviors.

The first ritual is forming a circle, a universal symbol that represents the notions of wholeness, timelessness, and all cyclic movement. A circle has no hierarchy, so everybody has a chance to really be with each other.

We pass around a talking stick for those who want to speak. We start the dialogue with questions: How are you feeling today? What happened this week? What are you hoping or expecting to do with your horse today? We all reflect and listen actively to each person's experience. Trust is very important, and it is understood that what is said in the circle is held sacred and not repeated off the ranch to others.

The second ritual to engage in a short meditation. The meditation is mostly to scan the body in a mindful way: to feel the feet on the ground, to check in with the heart and feel it beating. This helps the participants to experience a greater awareness within their bodies. The somatic aspect of this work is also important to the horse, because a horse responds to the energy and intention from the human. Horses will not be responsive if humans show up lost in their thoughts and not present with their heart.

Another ritual used is to have the veterans write down something that is holding them back, hurting them, or causing them to stumble. They look at what they wrote and, in their own way, say, "It served me when it served me." Then they toss the paper into a fire as an intention to let go of those fears and anxieties.

These rituals allow the veterans to slowly strip away the things that make them feel tight, isolated, and depressed. It helps them become more aware, and this awareness can be meaningful in releasing old patterns, creating new ones, and moving on, feeling lighter and more optimistic.

As we work with the veterans to start building more connection and focus on being present, they also learn how meaningful their energy can be.

Energy Exercises

Prior to meeting the horses, we introduce the veterans to exercises to help them be conscious of their energy fields. As prey animals, horses have an incredible sense about energy, so it's really important that each veteran learns to tune into his or her own field.

Our lessons are designed to demonstrate that we can send, direct, and receive energy—all within a field that can be felt but not seen—to create a connection.

This awareness of energy fields is important because people with PTSD, who are tired of feeling pain, tend to dissociate from their bodies. If the veterans can't understand the importance of staying physically and energetically within their bodies, they will have a more difficult time connecting with the horses. We want the veterans to make themselves available from their hearts.

Because of this need, we begin by having the veterans do energy- and body-awareness activities before meeting the horses.

> ***Exercise One: Recognizing pressure.*** In this exercise, we ask two veterans to hold a stick in place between their belly areas. They then move each other around the arena without talking, once with eyes open and once with eyes closed. Horses respond to pressure, and this gives the veterans an idea of how little pressure—called "feel" in horsemanship—it takes to make someone move. As an alternative, we ask them to hold on to reins so they can begin to feel the slightest tug or pull.

> ***Exercise Two: Recognizing the power of grounding and directing energy.*** Using partners, we ask the veterans to focus on a point in their head. Then we gently push their shoulders and show them how little it takes to lose their balance when we focus on the head space. Then we identify a point at the heart and again offer a slight push from behind. They notice that they can maintain their balance

when they focus on the heart. Finally, we ask them to focus on a point in their core area, and we gently push from behind again. This time, they barely move.

Exercise Three: Filling with Energy. These three demonstrations show that as their thoughts move around their body, so does their grounding. Horses notice this, so it's important that humans become aware of it as well.

Once the participants are aware of their grounded energy, we ask them to imagine filling their arms with water, like a firehose, and directing this energy far away. With their arms "full," they experience strength they had not been aware of before the exercise. Now they recognize how they can direct their energy.

We spend a lot of time helping the veterans tune into their own bodies. As they experience more about their own energy, they start to feel more alive and aware of the impact of energy on themselves and others. We always have a counselor on hand in case the somatic experiences trigger any particular responses that may need support.

Going With: Obstacle Training

Chapter 3

RECOGNIZING AND BUILDING A CONNECTION

Ray, Storm & Bianca

In one of our cohorts, we had a suicidal woman who worked with a wrangler named Ray and a horse named Storm. Ray was able to use his and Storm's energy awareness to help that veteran through a very rough period.

In her journal, Bianca (whose name we have changed to protect her privacy) wrote about how she hated everybody, that she cut herself, and that she had taken drugs and was thinking about using crystal meth again.

After Bianca spent a morning session glowering at every-one, Ray quietly said to her, "You're going to have as good a day as you want to have." She didn't respond immediately, but he made it clear that her experience was her responsibility.

During her time working with Ray and Storm, Bianca

decided that it would help her more if she made the decision to like herself. It wasn't easy, and she didn't change immediately, but that first wall had come down.

In fact, her very last journal entry included how much she appreciated Ray—and that he had contributed to saving her life.

You Choose the Horse and the Horse Chooses You

Before the veterans actually meet the horses, they often experience feelings of fear, worry, and anxiety.

Sometimes we forget how scared or anxious the veterans actually are. And sometimes they don't tell us until later that they are also worried none of the horses will like them, or they won't connect with any of the horses. To continue building trust, we have to address these fears.

First, we turn the horses out in the arena and spend time just watching them. We call this herd observation. It works better if we don't tell the story of each horse and just allow the veterans to observe and sense their own impressions of what may or may not be happening.

This is when we'll ask the veterans questions: Whom do you see as the dominant one? Whom are you attracted to? Why are you attracted to that horse? Is it because of the color, because it seems dominant, or because it came over to the fence and nuzzled you? The veterans can say anything they want, and we don't correct them about the horses or their personalities.

When the veterans start to feel a little more comfortable being in the presence of these large animals, each wrangler takes a horse. We walk the horses around the arena, going from person to person. Each veteran has a few minutes to put his or her hands on that horse, to walk around it, feel the horse, and process how they may or may not be making a connection with that horse.

We get to see some very magical moments when an immediate connection forms.

One woman, Ann, had an experience that was clear to everybody. Frosty, one of the program horses, nudged Ann away over to one side and just hugged her with his head and neck. He made it very clear that they would be working together! And they just loved each other the whole time.

A Connection Is Created

After everyone has had a few minutes with each horse, we have all the horses stand in the middle of the arena. Then I ask the veterans to go stand next to the horse they feel the most connection to.

Some people feel a connection because they like the color of the horse or because that horse came over and rubbed on them. Others feel it in their bodies or in their hearts, or they get the chills. One of the veterans, John, said that when he met his horse, Reggie, it was like an electric shock went through him. I've met horses that, when I touched them, made me feel like somebody just turned on the lights. With other horses, I don't even know if they're home. The lights are out, and there is no connection.

Sometimes, the person is totally oblivious that a horse is trying to get his or her attention. And that shows up in other areas of life too. The veteran doesn't realize that someone wants to have a relationship, or vice versa: the veteran wants a relationship with someone who doesn't want that relationship.

Some people say, "I don't know; I like them all," or "I didn't feel anything." If that happens, we may give them a horse that hasn't been chosen. They'll work with that horse, and they'll still get it!

The truth is, you can probably have a relationship with just about any horse if you open your heart to it. The horses are open to the connection. It's usually the humans who start to notice that they've turned themselves off, constructed boundaries, and shut their heart.

But once that connection is created, it gets stronger throughout the program.

In fact, one time I tried to shift Aaron, a veteran with PTSD and a traumatic brain injury, away from Rusty, because Rusty can be a little bit difficult. I gave Aaron another horse, and within a week he was back with Rusty. I had to tell Aaron, "Okay, we'll be really careful, but Rusty's not a good horse for you to take on a trail ride, so you'll have to stay around here and in the arena."

Aaron just smiled and said, "That's okay. I love Rusty, and I always feel better after I spend time with him."

Write It Out

After each session, there is a journal assignment for the veterans to do to reflect on their experiences and notice how it shows up in their lives.

For this session, the questions are as follows:

Identify one or two people whom you trust?

Think of a situation where you felt a tremendous sense of trust for another person or team?

Write about that person or situation that let you know your trust was well founded?

The effects of this newfound connection and feeling of trust aren't just in our heads. They show up physically as well.

We aren't going to discuss the data from the research after every chapter, but during this session, the autonomic nervous system significantly improves. The first time it's measured, the veterans are a little anxious. But now they show improvement, even from the beginning to the end of the session. This indicates that the veterans are starting to relax. They realize they're safe in the program. Their autonomic nervous system goes pretty quickly to a balance when they interact with the horses.

With a bond of trust starting to be built, we are one step closer to the aim of reducing the symptoms of PTSD and living wholeheartedly. But trust and connection are just the beginning. Chapter 3 teaches you to recognize and build on that connection.

The Magic of Connection

Bianca didn't just listen to Ray's words; she began to trust him. That trust was the basis of a connection for her—a connection to Ray, to Storm, and to her own life.

After beginning to build a feeling of trust, we go deeper toward the experience of connecting from the heart with a horse. The research on changing neuropathways shows that with greater awareness, it is possible to alter dysfunctional patterns that no longer serve a person. Veterans can establish new neuro-functions that contribute to more positive outcomes and happier living. They begin to extinguish the flames of anxiety, separateness, and some aspects of depression.

When the veterans first meet their horse, they start to feel a sense of connection. After they come back to the ranch for the second session, they usually want to go see the horse right away. They fill out their PANAS and take their HRV reading, but then they go right down to see their horse. They are anxious and excited to validate that what happened the previous week was real. When they walk toward their chosen horse, present in their hearts, the horse comes right over to them. And as soon as they see their individual horse, they recognize again the magic of connection.

Now we work to build on that sense of connection, to seek ways to help it grow. Participants continue to pay attention to the moment they experience that connection with their horse. This is done while grooming a horse, catching a horse, and being introduced to round pen work.

Grooming a Horse

When the veterans first work with their individual horses, we help each person go get his or her horse, halter it, lead it, and tie it up at a tie rail. We have them start to groom their horses, moving from a stiffer brush to softer ones and then to the face brush. We don't want anyone working from a basis of fear. Safety is our number one goal.

Many people rarely touch or hold others, except maybe their spouse or children. They worry about pulling a comb through a horse's mane or tail or how hard they have to press the brush to get the dirt off. As they experiment, though, they get that tactile feedback about how much pressure to use, and they feel pleasure from the experience. At the same time, the horse allows the veteran to touch it, and they continue to experience and validate meaningful connection.

When the veterans are grooming the horses, we ask a series of questions:

What do you notice about your horse?

What do you think your horse wants you to know?

The veterans might notice the horse indicating, Hey, would you scratch me under the neck?

Or, Gee, I feel really safe with you. Sure, you can pick my foot up.

While physically caring for another being, veterans feel something shift inside of them, especially if they haven't been able to practice self-care very well.

This experience isn't just about an animal standing there being groomed. It is the building of a relationship. Some of the veterans shed tears during this session because they realize their own authentic self for the first time in a long time, and with that comes a release of tension.

The physical movement of brushing creates a rhythm for the veteran and the horse. That motion also contributes to a release of trauma held in the body. The veterans relax and get comfortable with what is going on in their body and begin to reprogram new ways to manage anxiety and trauma.

As they groom, the veterans see the mane get soft and

how pretty the horses look when they are cleaned. The veterans have a visible representation of that connection and the energy they have given to another being.

Catching a Horse

Once the participants become comfortable with grooming, they feel empowered the next week to catch their horses themselves with minimal assistance from their wrangler.

Our approach is to empower the veterans: first demonstrating, then helping, then letting them do things for themselves. The first time the vets come to the ranch, their wrangler gathers their horse for them. The next time, we're with them as they approach and catch their horse with minimal supervision. After that, we may just observe them while they do most of it themselves. That leads up to when we can say, "Okay, go get your horse yourself."

The progression is important, because it leads to empowerment—at a safe, comfortable pace.

In our program, we work hard to ensure the veteran never feels like a failure for not being able to master a technique. We do not think it is helpful to put people in an unknown, uncomfortable, or potentially frightening situation and expect them to figure it out. That doesn't support the environment of safety and trust that is necessary.

Everything we do has a safety element to it, so we demonstrate the technique for how to hold a rope, how to approach the horse, and how to put the halter on safely. We have a reason for everything we do, but we also make allowances for each person's skill level. A technique can be modified as long as we keep safety in mind. Different people do things in different ways, and we want everyone to know that each person will master the skills if he or she shows up with an open heart.

We slowly begin to integrate technique with intuition to approach the horse with energetic awareness. Setting up that connection is part of the learning process. We use those teachable moments to help the veterans build that relationship each time they interact with their horses.

Round Pen Work

At some point during the session, the veterans start to go into a round pen—an enclosed circle fifty feet in diameter, used for training—with their horses. They remove the halter and learn to work their horse at liberty, meaning without ropes or tools. At that point, if the horse walks away and shows that it doesn't want to be with the veteran, it becomes obvious that a connection hasn't yet been built.

However, when the horse demonstrates that the connection exists, the veterans are ready to practice moving their horses using their own energy. We first show them the techniques of how to do that—not to just use the technique, but to *be* the energy. Then, as the veteran gains confidence, we back away. We're just there for support, and we ask the veterans, "Can you move the horse away from you? Can you get it to walk? Can you get the horse up to a trot? Can you turn it?"

I remember when my first wild horse and I started to get on the same page. When I was in the round pen one day, I thought to myself, I want him to go up into a canter, and he did it before I even lifted my hand. At first I thought I should reprimand him because he was going too fast, but then I realized I had transferred energy to him when I thought about cantering, and he read that in my body. In fact, one of my trainers always used to say, "Make your thoughts be their thoughts."

The veterans start to work on how to pay attention to those subtleties when they are with their horse. They learn to manage the ups and downs of their energy—how not to be too big, too little, or not there at all. They learn the nuances of slight changes in their body language and how much that means to their horse.

Then they draw back their energy and ask the horse to come to them. When they ask the horse to stop, it should look at them and then drop its head and lick and chew at the lips. That means the horse is comfortable, it's paying attention, and it's checking in with the veteran. Finally, the veteran approaches and pets the horse. Because they've created this connection together, the horse will walk off with its person—without a lead line.

The veterans are always astounded by that! It's a big moment when a horse walks with somebody because the two are connected energetically. That feeling leads to an opening of the heart, and the bond between horse and veteran continues to get bigger.

Write It Out

The journal assignment after this session is to pay attention when you are interacting with others. Questions were posed to the veterans to explore those interactions:

How much do you feel connected to them?

Is there warmth or coldness in the conversation?

Or do you not feel any connection at all?

When you meet new people, what happens to make you feel safe in their presence?

When you get together with those you care about, what do you observe?

We encourage the veterans to remember the positive feeling they have when they are with their horses, and then see if they can find that feeling with the people they reach out to.

One Vietnam veteran wrote, *"I never told my wife about Vietnam, and I started telling her a little bit. And wow, it changed the way we feel about each other, because that door was always shut."*

Another veteran said, *"I called my daughter, and we hadn't talked in three months, but we had a conversation and it was a lot easier."*

Another post-9/11 vet told us, *"I was thinking about Rusty, and it really helped me to talk to my daughter."*

Once a connection is built, many tell us they feel it can never be broken. One situation, however, that can challenge a person's newly connected or reconnected relationship is not showing up to maintain his or her half of the relationship. In the next chapter, we discuss how to sustain that new connection by learning to be present.

Getting Instruction on Presence and Feel

Chapter 4

SUSTAINING A
CONNECTION THROUGH
STAYING PRESENT

Dan and Shiloh

Dan is a veteran of the US Army post-9/11, and Shiloh is a
wild mustang Ellen adopted in 2000. This is Dan's story, in
his own words.

*I was riding Shiloh in the round pen, but even while
I was on his back, Shiloh kept walking over to Ellen.
After the third or fourth time this happened, my
frustration was obvious. I finally asked Ellen, "What's
going on with this horse?"*

*"You're going in and out of being here," she said.
"Shiloh is worried because you're not giving him any
direction. He's checking in with me and asking me for
help, because he knows I'm here."*

"Yeah," I nodded. "I've been really worried about

a lot of things, and I can't stop thinking about them.
I keep getting distracted by my own thoughts. I can't
believe a horse knows this!"

I tried riding for a few more minutes, but my mind
kept wandering, and I just couldn't concentrate. My
doctor had recently changed my meds, and it was
difficult to adjust.

I never was able to stay focused that day. I could tell
that Ellen felt bad because she wants everyone to have
positive experiences at each session. In the closing circle,
though, I mentioned that I understood the lesson and
really wanted to work on it. And as I reflected on it in
my weekly journal, I ended with, "Wow, imagine, I
learned about presence from a horse!"

The Gift of Presence

Building a connection is one of the main goals of the HEART
OF HORSEMANSHIP© program—and the building process continues throughout every session. We don't just stop working
on trust or stop connecting and move on to something else.
Everything builds on the heart connection.

This next session is about sustaining that connection
and learning to stay present for a longer period of time.
Those with PTSD often get caught in spinning thoughts
about the past and worry about the future. Working with
horses helps veterans be present and mindful because a

horse will give immediate feedback as to how well one is doing with this.

At this stage, the veteran no longer simply recognizes the connection; he or she begins to ramp up awareness and learns to sustain that connection. When the connection isn't there, the horse will likely walk away and ignore the person. But when the connection is really strong and the person is aware of it, it's energetic. The veterans describe it as magnetic.

In horsemanship language, this is referred to as a feel. We start learning about feel and timing when working with others. We ask the veterans,

> "What can you do to be really aware of how you show up and stay there, even as other things happen around you?"

A big reason that it's important to stay present is for safety—mainly emotional safety.

Horses depend on herd hierarchy and leadership. The human is the leader and is mandated to keep the herd members safe. So part of sustaining a connection is about leading—not dominating, but partnering and supporting the horse. When people bounce in and out of their awareness, in their heads and in their hearts, it's very uncomfortable for horses. They perceive their human as being unsafe and not leading.

Ultimately, when working with horses, humans are responsible for the relationship and for providing safety to their horse—and to the people in their lives.

For this session, the veterans will spend most of the time working at liberty with their horse, with the goal of finishing their session feeling better than when they started, which prepares them to work with others.

At Liberty

To help anchor the ability to be present, the veterans spend most of this session in the round pen or the arena working at liberty, with no lead ropes or physical attachments to their horse.

The round pen work is profoundly powerful. If the participants cannot learn to work with their horse in a connected way from the ground, then they will not be allowed to mount and ride their horse. They focus on keeping their attention on their horse, asking them to walk, trot, and canter, then make transitions in speed up and down, ending with what is known as a joining together. The veterans direct their energy as they ask their horse to make each transition.

Even if they are not working at liberty for this part, they still direct their energy. They might pick up the lead line and, with the line left slack and the horse walking next to their shoulder, look at an obstacle and intentionally direct the horse to step over it. The horse doesn't understand if they just command, "Step over it!"

If the veteran has to tug on the line, it might reveal a weak or nonexistent connection, and he or she may need to work on focusing on the present moment.

When the horse stops, turns, and licks its lips, it is a positive sign of the electricity that is shared and the beginning of recognizing connection.

When the veteran asks the horse to follow him or her, the horse will follow if the connection is there. The horse will walk with the veteran, and, at times, it may seem like the horse is even dancing in synchronicity. When this happens, the veteran often experiences a momentous shift. Many report a warm and satisfying sensation in their heart. Some have a few tears of joy, and many display smiles that have not been seen that big in years.

This is one of our favorite aspects of the program. Many other horsemanship programs that do not involve riding will work with this connection on the ground and build on it. We find that most of the veterans have the goal of riding, so we make an extra effort to prepare them to have that same heart experience when they mount their horse. We also make sure our horses are safe and responsive to the level of rider so that we do not put the veterans at risk or challenge their fears in a way that is not helpful to their healing.

Better Than You Began

As veterans build their relationship with the horse, they begin to realize that anything that happens between them and their horse is due to human communication and not because it is a "bad" horse.

We can't get mad at the horse or blame it when something goes wrong. Horses don't have the processing capability to set us up or manipulate us. So we don't want to project our anger or frustration onto another being.

To use an example from my own life, my horse Rusty got out of his stall yesterday because I hadn't closed it properly. He went into the barn and made a huge mess and then wandered around the property. When I found him, I felt angry and had an unfamiliar urge to scold him. But then I saw how much grain he ate and thought, "Oh wow, he could get really sick. I hope he's not going to colic."

Whom was I really mad at? Myself. I had not secured his stall properly. I hadn't expected him to get out, and I also had not shut the barn. It wasn't his fault. He was just being Rusty.

Sometimes when we work with the veterans, we'll see the horse running in the round pen with its head up in the air. The veteran has probably projected too much energy at the horse and is not clearly communicating his or her intentions. The person working with the horse may become frustrated and want to say, "Okay, I'm done." But it is not okay to put the horse away in that state of mind.

Instead, we help veterans find a place where they and their horse are in a good place together. We encourage them to look for places to finish the session feeling connected. When the horse's ears are forward, tail is relaxed, and face is soft, nice things are happening in the relationship. And we always help the veterans look to find that moment of softness happening between them and their horses.

We build on those moments where they want to be together and not say goodbye. If they end on a good note, then they will start on a good note next time they meet.

Working with Others

Just like we always want to leave the horses better than we found them, we want the veterans to feel confident as well.

A lot of the veterans we work with take medications that make it harder to sustain that presence because their minds keep ping-ponging around. This is where mindfulness and meditation can really help to quiet and calm their minds so that they *are* able to be present.

As people start to witness their own emotional landscape, they see how difficult their relationships have been because they are not fully present. This shows up particularly as they begin to feel what it's like to work with others again.

Many of the veterans return the following week surprised by how much more fulfilling their interactions have become within their significant relationships. The nonjudgmental feedback from their horse translated into the need to pay more attention to encounters between themselves and others. After recognizing the pleasant feelings following connection with their horse, the veterans truly want to experience a better connection with people; they want to transfer that experience to their relationships with their fellow humans.

Horses facilitate veterans feeling safe enough to open up about what is going on. Working with a nonjudgmental sentient being helps build that confidence muscle.

At the conclusion of this kind of session, one of the veterans told us, *"I'm talking a little bit more when I feel bad, instead of closing up."* Other veterans from the rehabilitation center said they were inspired to clean up their communication with people outside of their program.

One of the Vietnam veterans showed up at the following session pleased with how he was fixing his marriage because of his experience working with Shiloh. He felt less scared to express his feelings, and he was amazed at how much happier his wife was. In fact, she encouraged him to go work with the horses as often as he could.

Write It Out

What do you notice about yourself—your thoughts, the feelings in your body, the emotions that come up—when you are with another person or in a group situation?

How connected do you feel?

Do you notice when that connection is strong or weak, like with your horse?

How have your observations changed from this week to last week?

What is the difference between noticing a connection and then consciously maintaining a connection?

With that strong connection in place, you and your horse partner are learning to work together.

Aaron is a veteran with a traumatic brain injury from an improvised explosive device (IED). Here, in his own words, he shares the importance of being present.

After connecting with a horse, it makes it easier to connect with other human beings. And you feel that connection without judgment.

A lot of not wanting to connect with other human beings is because you don't want to get close to somebody because you're afraid it's going to change, or they're going to die, or they'll hurt you.

When I first came to the program and started feeling close to Rusty, it was very much like, "Whoa, this program is going to leave, and I'm not going to be able to be around this horse." And it took me back to the military, where you get close with all these guys and then deployment ends. Or they die. Or they commit suicide. And you're on your own again.

So I made a decision. I told myself, You know what? I'm just going to enjoy the time I have with this horse. And when it's over, I'll enjoy the memory of the time that I had with him. I realize it's just the seasons of life—and seasons change.

During this same period, I realized I was learning to do the same thing with my dad. We knew he had a terminal illness, so each time I'd go back to visit, I knew that it might be the last. I wanted to bond with him in hopes of getting things right with him before he passed away. We'd had some rough times while I was having some mental problems, and we got in some big fights. But we were able to reconnect and smooth those things over in the end. And Rusty helped with that, because it's easier now to say goodbye.

Even when I look at my daughter, I know that she's getting ready to be a teenager, so it'll be time to say goodbye to her childhood. But again, with Rusty I realize this is another season of life.

Chapter 5

GOING TOGETHER

Mama K & Shiloh

Mama K is Aaron's caregiver, and she is also a veteran medic. This is her story.

One cool, windy day, just a couple of us were in the round pen. I was brushing Tonopah and Cougar with long, gentle strokes. Ellen looked over and asked me, "Why aren't you riding?"

I started to answer, "Well . . . "

That's when Ellen had an idea. "Why don't you ride Shiloh bareback? I'll be on one side, and Ray will be on the other. If you don't like it, we'll stop, and you can get off. But I want you to feel the horse, because it's a completely different feeling when you don't have stirrups and you're in direct contact."

Before I could say, "I'm doing what?" I was up on Shiloh without a saddle. I didn't even have time to get into my head and think about being scared—I just did it. Later, when I did have time to think about it, I realized how much trust I have in Ellen and Ray. I knew they wouldn't ask me to do anything I wasn't ready for—and that was worth every fear.

I could feel my heart open, and it opened a little bit more because this big, beautiful, powerful animal allowed me to sit right on his back. I felt like I knew Shiloh better after feeling his back and his muscles and his power and capability. Ellen took a picture of me, which I sent to my sister. My sister said, "Wow, you look so confident—I'm not going to worry about you anymore!"

Ellen saw something in me that I didn't see.

Going Together

I may have seen something in Mama K, but it was up to her to really *feel* it.

At this stage of the program, the veterans understand that riding a horse means to ride *with* a horse. We call that going together. And you have to have a relationship with your horse before you can really go together.

Unless we are in an intimate relationship, we often do not have the opportunity to feel the flow of energy with another. It may be something felt during team sports, training, or combat. Feeling this flow of energy from one another is critical to good horsemanship.

Going together requires the veteran to maintain a connection with the horse.

It's like dancing! You don't want to be stiff and rigid, because then the horse will become stiff and rigid. If you want to dance together and do the tango, you have to go with somebody. You have to trust the leader and know that he or she is not going to get you in trouble or let you fall to the ground.

As you relax into that movement and rhythm with the horse, you and the horse both look for that oneness. You'll get it little by little, and you'll feel a softening within yourself as you connect more and more.

In this session, veterans learn the tools to "go together"—including saddling and beginning to ride their horse at a walk. The focus is on building trust, as well as on gaining and keeping the connection. However, the stakes go up a little as, riding our horses, we build our awareness around the flow of working with another being.

The Gear

One thing we really didn't anticipate was just how interested the veterans would be in learning about the different gear used in riding. They have a lot of gear and equipment in the military, and they often have to learn a lot about it and know what each part does.

That practice of learning is evident with the riding gear

as well. The veterans see the gear and want to know how it works. They want to know when we use each of the different halters, bits, helmets, and saddles, or why saddles are shaped differently. They examine the stirrups and practice how to lower and raise them. They figure out how to work clasps, buckles, and bits. One group wanted to know why different sets of chaps look different or cover more leg.

We see some of this interest when we first start to groom the horses, but it really goes up a level as we talk about saddles, bridles, and the gear used for riding. We don't want to flood the veterans with information, so sometimes we wait for them to ask.

For example, the veterans often haven't started to separate out the difference in why Storm has one bridle, Sassy has another, and Shiloh has a completely different one. I know why, because I know their mouths, but new riders may not know to ask that.

The participants want to know specifically the impact on the horse of a certain piece of gear and how it contributes to a better connection. They now realize that everything involved in working with horses is about connecting, maintaining connection, directing their horse, and communicating with it from a position of partnership, not dominance.

Those questions are great, and we're always happy to answer them in as much detail as people want to hear, because it means the veterans are engaged.

That's when we know that they're not just curious about

riding horses. Our participants are interested more and more in good horsemanship.

Get in the Saddle

Once we've discussed the gear, it's time to get the veterans in the saddle! (That is, of course, if and when each veteran is ready to take it to the next level.)

When they begin to sit on and ride a horse and sense their connection with it, the veterans are guided to concentrate on noticing where each hoof is and what it's doing. Their body tunes in to the horse and starts to develop more feel. When people sit in the saddle and walk their horses, they are asked to respond to the recognition of where each hoof is: "Tell us when the back left foot starts to lift off the ground."

At first, they struggle to sense their body in relationship to their horse. So while they ride, we'll help signal: "Now . . . and now . . . and now!"

In many ways, the horse's feet become their feet. When they notice how their legs shift and rock as the horse moves, they begin to feel a synchronicity between themselves and the horse. The session is accomplished at a walk with a constant focus on how the horse is moving and what that means to the veterans and their bodies.

As it turns out, the movement of the horse can be very soothing at a peaceful walk. The veterans learn to relax their bodies to help the horse relax as well. We help them focus on breathing and loosening tight muscles. Many of the veterans have a lot of injuries they don't like to talk about, and they hurt. However, after they get off the horse, they'll often say, "I feel so much better," or "I feel looser. My back doesn't hurt."

And when we see that someone is going through something, struggling with pain, or being triggered, it's important that they ride. The movement of the horse often helps them relax as well as let go of trauma held in their body.

Recently, Rich, a Vietnam veteran, was triggered after he brought his grandson out to a rodeo with our group one night. We had been harassed by a drunk guy, and we rehashed the experience during the next opening circle. Talking about the situation brought back the feelings of frustration and anger Rich had experienced. He wasn't able to say very much in the opening circle, but he did say he probably wasn't going to ride—he would just groom Shiloh.

But that trauma had been triggered, and we recognized that it needed to be released. Work by Peter Levine and other trauma experts has revealed that physical movement, particularly from walking and riding a horse, can help with releasing trauma. We encouraged Rich to at least get on and walk, just to let the horse move him and get that rhythm— and to release the cyclical thoughts going round and round about his anger over the drunk person's invasion.

By the end of the session, Rich had undergone a major

shift. He smiled and spoke up freely in the closing circle. In his words: *"I feel good right now. I came here feeling irritated, then I got depressed. I wasn't going to ride, and then after I spent some time with Shiloh, I started feeling better. And then I decided to ride—and I'm glad I did."* He felt connected. And he had a softness about him. That's somebody who has let go of trauma.

An Exchange of Energy

If I could, I would start everybody bareback—just like I did with Mama K in the session you read about at the beginning of this chapter. Unfortunately, many of the veterans are physically unable to sit on a horse bareback. However, for those who can, the experience helps them to relax their legs more and develop a stronger feel for and with their horse.

When you ride a horse, you feel the flow of energy differently than when you walk it, or groom it, or are just near a horse. Part of that is because you are on top of the horse instead of standing next to it. People who ride therapeutically may have felt diminished at one point. But sitting up that high gives you a new sense of power—and a new point of view. The world looks different from atop a horse.

It's also a little scary. The first time Aaron—the veteran who told his story in chapter 4—got on Rusty, he said, *"This is just enough fear for me. I used to like the adrenaline rush from riding my motorcycle, but since I got hurt, I have a lot of fear. There's still fear here, but it's something I can manage."* Being up high, on this big, powerful animal, can help you manage fear. And exchanging energy with your horse makes you both feel good! Sometimes, when you feel like you're just not getting anywhere, if you are able to relax and open your heart, you'll feel a surge of gratitude or appreciation. When that happens, it's actually a chemical reaction; your body is releasing serotonin and oxytocin. You might think to yourself, I'm tired of feeling lousy all the time. This feels pretty good!

Through this program, and through equine-partnered experiences, you can get that feeling without taking an antidepressant. That chemical reaction doesn't always have to come from a pill. It can happen naturally because of this connection.

Those of us who manage the program are not doctors. And this program does not endorse people going off their meds without a doctor's permission. However, our research has shown that the autonomic nervous system comes into balance when a person safely and mindfully works with horses. People feel better psychologically and emotion-ally—something antidepressants aim to do. That is why we spent several years conducting evidence-based research to help position equine therapy as a viable complementary approach to treating veterans with PTSD.

With or without other medication, a good dose of riding it out always seems to make people feel better.

Write It Out

In this session, we work on going together with another—building on trust, making a connection, sustaining a connection, and now moving forward together.

How does this translate to your human interactions during the week and your responses to symptoms around PTSD?

When you have time, reflect on what it was like to work with your horse and how often during the session you felt like you were "in the zone" together. What did that feel like?

Then look at your relationships and observe whether you have similar "zone" experiences with friends or family—perhaps even strangers. Does it feel satisfying?

Uncomfortable?

Motivating?

Challenging?

Scary?

Loving?

Does it provide a feeling of oneness?

Something else entirely?

Veterans are welcome to write about any other observations and experiences that come up for you.

In fact, completing this journal assignment prepares veterans for the next step. Chapter 6 is about communicating with confidence.

Around this point in the program, we see significant changes in the veterans—physiologically and mentally.

They may not even fully notice it yet, but we see their tolerance levels go up and their anxiety levels go down. They may not notice it because sometimes they get so used to feeling bad that they are not used to *not* feeling bad.

In this week, through the veterans self-reports, we see a bump in how veterans feel. They start to mention feeling good. They start to say, *"I feel good and I kind of like this!"*

Chapter 6

COMMUNICATING WITH CONFIDENCE

Paul & Maggie

Paul is a Navy veteran, and Maggie is a thoroughbred former race horse.

During one session, I was working in the round pen with one of the wranglers, Ray.

Ray said, "Walk your horse to the pole over there, turn around, and then come back."

I immediately thought, "That'll be easy to do."

I squeezed her flanks, but Maggie would not move forward. It was so frustrating, and I didn't know what to do.

I had been so excited about getting to the pole and back that, in my mind, we had already done it. Maggie, however, didn't get the message. As Ray put it, "You were already at that pole, but you left your horse behind—even though you were sitting on it."

*I tried to argue a little with Ray, but Ray just said,
"Paul, you need to ride your horse."*

"I am riding!" I said.

*And, technically, I was right—I was sitting on top
of that horse. But I wasn't in charge.*

A Relationship in Bloom

The old saying goes, "You ride the horse you lead." As Paul saw, if that partnership or heart connection is weak, things will not be as satisfying between horse and rider.

In chapter 4, we talked about staying present. That remains throughout the whole program, but it really blossoms here as the veteran continues to practice presence and shows up to lead. This allows that relationship to deepen.

This is the halfway point of the program. By now, we're pressing the veterans a little more firmly to consistently show up, provide direction for their horse, and get into a mastery point of view. When this begins to unfold, the veterans find themselves relaxing and enjoying their horses, each other, and the group experience.

The veterans still must make a point of being mindful, but the right things are now happening with less effort. Rather than worrying about how to stop their horse or move the horse forward, the veterans are finding that the technique has become familiar enough to do it softly, without self-consciousness or constantly making themselves stay in the moment. We start to move more from technique to feel. New neural pathways that contribute to more positive outcomes become established, creating a new norm for the veterans.

At this stage, we might drill deeper with each veteran to reflect on the relationship with his or her horse and discover what is and isn't working. We ask our participants, "What do you notice?"

They are also ready to work at the next level of horsemanship. They realize that working with horses is not so simple, and they now are able to handle more detail in their approach. New areas of concern arise: How do they manage their hands? Where are their elbows? Are their shoulders tense? How is their seat? How much leg pressure are they applying to work with their horse?

The veterans seem to thrive and not get confused by this increase in detail and skill—something that would not have happened the first day of the program.

In this chapter, we're going to give an overview of the skills needed to communicate gently with the horse and the ability to lead confidently.

How to Speak Horse

Before you can start to work with horses, just like with any relationship, you need to learn to understand what they're saying. Horses may speak their own language, but if you know the translation, you can see that they share a lot of the same messages we do. Instead of speaking with their mouths, horses communicate through their eyes, ears, tails, and bodies.

Horses can have soft eyes or hard eyes, just like we can. When we're mad, our eyes are fierce. And when we look at somebody with kindness and love, our eyes reflect a softness. When horses are anxious, they have hard eyes. But when they're in the zone, they get this faraway, soft look.

A horse's ears can also tell you a lot. If a horse has its ears turned back, it's upset. But if you're riding a horse and its ear comes back a little and turns toward you, it means the horse is listening to you and paying attention. When the horse's ears are forward and relaxed, you know the horse is happy.

When a horse swishes its tail, if it's not shooing away flies, then it usually means the horse is anxious and irritated.

Horses also release a lot of energy through their feet and mouths. Sometimes they stamp their feet because they are impatient or they want something to happen. When horses drop their heads, they release a chemical like serotonin or oxytocin that relaxes them. As prey animals, they're very vulnerable when they have their heads down to eat, so a dropped head shows trust and feelings of safety. Dropping their head, chewing, and licking releases some of the tightness in their muscles so their whole head, jaw, and neck relax.

Similar to humans, tight muscles and tension in their bodies mean the horse is stressed. When you see softness and relaxation throughout their bodies and faces, it means they are at ease. If you know what to look for and what it means, it will be easier to communicate with your horse partner.

Confidence

One of the most important goals at this point in the program is for the veterans to gain confidence in both horsemanship skills and their relationship with their horse.

The technical aspect of brushing and grooming horses is pretty easy to master. It's not that hard to pick up a brush and figure out how to get dirt off a horse. It's harder to recognize when the horse is comfortable and responsive as well as appreciative. Working at liberty feels safe and comfortable, and it allows appreciation and gratitude to grow between the veterans and their horses, solidifying that human-animal bond.

However, when we shift to the riding, some of the veterans are quite surprised at the amount of skill it takes to do good work with their horse. As stated earlier, mounting their horses causes a shift in the entire relationship. We do not let them ride their horse until it is evident to them and to us that a strong connection exists.

It may seem obvious, but one thing to remember is to breathe.

When we get scared, we tend to hold our breath and tighten our bodies. This can cause the horse to hold its breath too, thus creating tension between horse and rider. As the human relaxes, the horse relaxes. And we see that with the veterans: we watch their bodies, and we see how rigidly they sit on top of the horses. But as soon as the veterans start to breathe, that rigidity relaxes, and their relationship gets softer.

Yes, they need skills, but it's not only about technique. We want all of our participants to have confidence in what they're doing and in that connection they have with their horse.

Leadership

Horses are always asking, "Are you leading, or am I?" And with horses, it is your responsibility, as their leader, to take care of them. They are big animals, much stronger than us, and it can be dangerous to let them do what they want. Although they seem like gentle pets, they are big and can be unpredictable by nature.

My mentor used to say, "I want my horse to think I'm the most important thing in the world when he is with me." I agree. I don't want my horse to look around at trees or whinny to its friends. I want my horse to realize, "Ellen's safety depends on me, and I need to pay attention." When people expect that of their horses, they continue to build a strong bond.

Some of the veterans struggle quite a bit to build that kind of relationship with their horse. They may have had a lot of leadership experience in the military, but some of that may have waned in civilian life. Yet in our program, they have to show up, and they have to lead. And every single one of them has to learn to provide that sense of safety to the horse by taking care of it. Because when someone—horse or veteran—feels safe, he or she is able to trust more and show up for these activities with hearts open.

Sometimes people get frustrated when we point out, "Hey, your horse is dragging you," or "He's eating grass, and you don't even notice that he's not paying attention to you." But we always offer encouragement: "You can change that right here and now."

You can bring that horse into partnership with you right now. You don't have to go study the theory of partnership or think about it. You just have to find that connection inside you. Stop and take a deep breath. Think about how it feels for you, somatically, to be in connection with this horse. What does it feel like for that horse to pay attention to you? And when you find your moment of togetherness, you can move forward with a heartfelt connection.

Often, people can make those shifts right then and

there. Sometimes, we see a complete change in participants within five minutes. They can change what happens in their body, and they can apply that new perception of leadership to civilian life: this is what it feels like to be in charge, without being mean, but bringing this horse with me in a soft way, in partnership, to accomplish a job.

That feeling doesn't always sustain itself, but once the veteran has identified what it feels like to be a good leader, a different feeling or concept than before, then there is always that quest with the horse to find that sweet spot together. It is very empowering and purposeful.

Write It Out

At this point, we see changes show up in the research. The veterans self-report a higher level of happiness with themselves, less anxiety, and more optimism about their future. They consistently report a general sense of overall well-being.

In this week's journal activity, participants are asked to:

Observe what unfolds this week, and then, in your journal, apply these skills and abilities to the relationship with yourself and others.

Write about what you notice as a result of your work from this chapter.

We are more than halfway through this journey to feeling wholehearted. The next chapter will be another shift to accessing more aliveness in their bodies.

Paul & Maggie, Part Two

Remember Paul's story from the beginning of this chapter?

Well, after that ride—when we were all debriefing in a group—Paul reflected on his situation with Maggie. "Wow, that happens to me in my relationships, too. My dates blow me off, just like Maggie blows me off. I've been going to therapy once a week, and I never learned that much in all those sessions!"

When Paul came back the following week, he told the group, "I had a date, and it went really well. Working with Maggie inspired me to take that feeling of living in the moment and be present in all the relationships I have with people. I feel like that's really changed my relationships with people, in general. It's helped me connect a lot better—with people and horses!"

Paul now shows up weekly, and he's really *there*. He's a smart guy with great ideas, and he's becoming a true leader. We've seen a big change in his horsemanship, and now he seems much more confident, too.

Making the First Openhearted Connections

Chapter 7

Finding Aliveness in
Your Body

Sean & Maggie

Sean, whose name has been changed, is a veteran from the
residential treatment center who participated in one of our
first cohorts of the program. He'd had problems with alco-
hol on top of—or because of—dealing with his PTSD. He
wasn't quite aware of who he was or what was happening in
his heart. And he didn't smile—*ever*.

But we could see that Sean had more to find in himself,
so we facilitated his connection to a horse called Maggie.
We knew that if he stayed on the ground, he was never
going to get any further.

And by just walking with her—it wasn't a motorcycle,
it wasn't a race car, it was just a horse walking along, with
him on her back—Sean smiled! Later, he said that's when
he realized he had a connection with this animal. He felt a
freedom he hadn't felt before.

He had a hard time articulating his relationship with a horse, but Sean said simply, "I look forward to seeing Maggie each week. And that makes me not want to drink, because I know that if I do, I won't be able to come back." That connection made Sean feel he could do something else with his life. It made him feel alive.

A Flow of Energy

The connection that Sean felt was so strong and joyful because he had that first experience of being open, energetically.

When riding a horse, it is helpful to have what is called an active seat so that you can feel and work with an awareness of energy within the body to communicate direction to the horse.

When people get on a horse the first few times, they often sit like they are on a bike or a motorcycle, or even the couch. Horses can sense when humans are not aware of the energy in their body, their posture, and their subtle movements. It is also apparent if humans are daydreaming and not focusing on the present moment. They look like a sack of potatoes up on a horse, and they just let the horse carry them around, offering no leadership or direction.

We want the veteran to be able to relax and enjoy the horse-human relationship. Working in a heartfelt way leads to more confidence, less anxiety, more connection, less isolation, and learning the skills to better manage negative emotions. When they work energetically with their body, the veterans gain the ability to become more open, to connect to their horse, and to share comfort in movement.

If you saw Ray, one of our wranglers, ride a horse, you would think he and his horse shared the same body. They just fit! It's like putting your hand in a glove. Just looking at them makes you think, "That's a good pair." They move together and communicate well, and the horse is responsive. As a cowboy himself, Ray looks effortless in his skill working with his horse, Duro.

That is the flow you ultimately want to experience. It is like water flowing, and you can't dam it up. You just go with it.

But Ray has been riding his whole life, and most of the veterans are with us for only eight weeks or so. At this stage, they are just gaining tiny insights into this experience of flow and connection with their horse. As it grows, they start to find aliveness. By this session, the veteran has the skill, knowledge, and ability to ask more from the horse and work for longer segments in a partnership capacity.

We teach participants to use a very simple approach, often called CPR-R, to work with their horse in a way that makes sense to them, one with an element of structure and discipline. With this approach, the veterans are better able to direct their horses, pay attention to the amount of energy they use, and recognize the reaction and performance of themselves and their horses.

CPR-R: Cue, Pressure, Response, and Release

Good horsemanship is about feel and timing. To work on these skills, we introduce CPR-R: cue, pressure, response, and release.

The *cue* is what you want your horse to do. Maybe you indicate, "I'd like you to drop your head." So you then pick up the reins, and add a little *pressure*, which is an aspect of feel. As soon as the horse gives you the desired *response* of softness, you *release* the pressure. It is easier said than done, and many good horsemanship people spend their whole lives perfecting the timing and feel of this with their horse.

As veterans work on the connection with their horse using this approach, they may get to the stage where they barely pick up the reins, the horse drops its head immediately, and the veteran offers a quick release from the pressure. Doing this over and over, and getting it more precise, offers a tuning and sensitivity to others that helps the veteran be more successful in relationship interactions.

To get this to work effectively, however, requires timing.

Every horse has a different point of softness, so we are always aiming to offer that softness, that point of release— that timing. This is everything to the horse. A horse responds to pressure. So if you push your horse and it moves and you don't release the pressure but continue to push it, the horse is going to think it needs to do more and more. But if you say, "I'd like you to side-pass," then release as soon as the horse takes one step, it knows it got the right answer. Participants learn to build on those small steps.

Often, I see people who have decided that the horse doesn't want to come with them. So, they pull and tug; in other words, they put a lot of pressure on their horse. The horse still doesn't come, so, out of frustration, the rider lets go. This trains the horse to do the wrong thing because the rider thinks, "Oh, that didn't work," and then releases the pressure. The horse thinks, "Wow, that must have been the right answer since there no longer is any pressure on me!" So the horse has learned to get the release, and now it will repeat that behavior again and again until it is trained differently.

Once you get in the game, you have to stay there. So if you add a little pressure and that horse doesn't come with you, you don't need to add too much more pressure, but you do need to find a way to get that response. Find some softness and then release, so your horse can get the right answer. The biggest thing to remember with timing is to be careful when you release, because you will get that response again next time.

Like life itself, it takes patience and emotional management to competently follow the cue-pressure-response-release.

How You Show Up

Not only do we want the veteran to be able to learn to direct their horse, but we want them to do so meaningfully and with purpose.

It becomes important, from when they first go up to the horse until they put them away, that participants maintain an awareness of the impact of their energetic self on their horse. We find that the veterans smile more, laugh, and talk with their horses as this awareness grows. A lot of joy comes from the exchange of energy, and the veterans speak of feeling more alive than they have for a long time.

One Marine Corps veteran said, *"I have not felt this good inside for a long time. I like being able to work with my horse and know precisely what is going on with him. It helps me feel more confident in what I am taking in around me and not be so paranoid. It is so easy for me to know that what I am doing or communicating with my horse is working, because the response is so real and authentic. It has helped me back at the center to have more confidence and insight when I talk with people."*

As they work with their horses, veterans begin to manage how much to dial up their energy or, alternatively, dial it down. They transfer this awareness to deciding how much energy and direction they offer while sitting on their horse to move it and stop it.

Learning this with a horse first gives veterans some validation, because horses won't lie about how their human partners show up. When veterans show up with a sense of themselves as a physical, spiritual, and emotional being, it indicates to the horse that their human partners are present, that they want to engage with their horse, and that they are ready to move with it.

How to Stay Awake in the Body

We have talked about how each session of the program and each chapter of this book builds on the previous. An aspect of that building is the ability to become more comfortable with who the veteran is, to feel safe with his or her feelings and emotions. This helps veterans gain skills and confidence in life decisions.

It's okay to have PTSD, to have anxiety, to truly understand the upheaval that anxiety causes, and to be able to look at it, watch it, and manage it.

Horses give really accurate feedback, so when the veterans get to this stage, they start to put the pieces together and focus on improving a lot of their personal life skills. Part of that skill is just to show up for themselves and others. And then they start to be conscious of themselves: "Here I am, physically, emotional, spiritually." Physically, they might notice that their left shoulder is tight today, so they focus on relaxing it so as not to contribute to their horse feeling tight. Emotionally, they realize that their heart feels full, and they reach out to pet their horse. Spiritually, something has evolved for them that is real and connected—something bigger than themselves.

The veterans begin to take care of themselves on all levels and, in turn, are able to reach out and care for others without fear, anxiety, or triggering emotional upheavals.

One post-9/11 Air Force veteran stated, "Wow, this is really taking ahold in me. I can step back a little bit and not be afraid of myself. With Shiloh, he is so honest and open and bighearted that I feel more settled in my life than I have for a long time."

Write It Out

For this journal assignment the veterans were asked to reflect on the journey thus far. They were instructed to keep in mind the focus of each session and their progress on the path! The questions posed were:

Where and when do you experience moments of wholeheartedness with yourself and others?

What are you doing or feeling when these moments happen?

Is this related to how you work with your horse—always feeling for the lightness and adjusting the energetic feel?

Several veterans responded to this assignment with reflections such as, "This program has saved my life. I never thought it was possible to regain that sense of joy and optimism. I have been carrying around the shame and nightmares from Vietnam for fifty years. Horses, particularly my buddy Shiloh, make life feel good again."

You may notice that you also feel more alive, in your body and energetically. Now's not the time to rest: we must continue building on that feeling! In chapter 8, the connection Veterans made evolves into confident performance while working together with their horse.

Celebration

WORKING TOGETHER IN CONFIDENT PERFORMANCE

Jimmy's Story

Jimmy, one of the Vietnam vets in our program, loves all the horses. The following is his story:

He's older, and he has some health problems, so he doesn't ride much. But he loves to brush the horses, and he feels good just being around them. Sometimes, he will work on leading one of the horses as they walk together around the arena.

On one of his first days in the program, the wranglers kept coaching him, "You need to look up, not down, when you're leading a horse."

He's very mellow, so he nodded and kept going. During the closing circle, he said, "I don't think I'm going to make a very good horse person. I had three people tell me today to look up when I'm walking this horse."

I nodded and said, "Well, yes, you need to see where you're going, and the horse needs you to provide leadership."

"But I can't look up," he said. "If I do, people will get killed."

When we talked more, we discovered that he was a highly decorated Vietnam veteran. And one of his jobs had been to disarm IEDs, so for him, looking at the ground meant looking for signs that anything might be unsafe or blow up. And he'd been doing that for fifty years!

"Nothing is going to blow up here," we promised him. "And if you need to walk along looking down, don't worry about it."

He was so distraught that we worried he might not even come back.

But the next week in the closing circle, he smiled and said, "I don't need to look down anymore."

With his horse, with his group—with his herd—he finally felt safe enough to look up and forward.

Where the Hooves Meet the Dirt

Jimmy got what he needed out of the experience—not necessarily from one horse, but from being around horses and his group of veterans, and from learning to lead a horse in partnership.

And that's what this chapter is about—working together in confident performance.

When we say performance, we're not talking about

putting on a show or getting a blue ribbon. We mean that you and your horse become a high-performing partnership. And that means that you both have a job to do—even if it's just riding to one point in the arena and back. Like humans, horses feel better when they have a sense of purpose.

I worry about some of the veterans who are put on medical leave and then feel like they don't have value or don't make a difference. They feel like they have no purpose. For example, one of our veterans, Christine, was put on medical leave and was left with nothing to do. She felt like she was just killing time between sessions, saying, "This program is my anchor to the world. I look forward to Mondays for the first time ever! And then my week is over, and I'm just looking forward to the next time I can be with Storm."

She felt so adrift that she came out and mucked the stalls, just to have something to do and to feel better about herself.

People need to be given purpose, and horses do, too. You have to give your horse a job! That gives both of you purpose. Your job is to create this relationship by doing something together.

In this chapter, we direct the veterans to work with their horse from a sense of purpose and help them find their herd.

Work with a Purpose

Most of what we do—in the **HEART OF HORSEMANSHIP**© program and in life—has purposeful behavior. That's what we get to in this session: performing is real-life purposing.

While the veterans walk with their horses around the round pen, we might have them lead the horses over an obstacle course. That gives both them and the horse a task to accomplish. The veterans are not sitting on the couch watching TV, eating chips, and drinking beer. They have a job to do with their horse, and that is to go through this obstacle course.

Or we might set up a box with water in it and ask the veterans to walk through the water with their horses. To do this job, the veterans can't cajole their horse or swat it or pull it. Instead, they have to support the horse to feel good inside, so it trusts them enough to be able to take a step and know it won't be led into danger. When a horse looks at a water box, it's scary. Horses don't have good depth perception, and they don't understand why they have to walk through the water box when they can easily walk around it.

All of these obstacles are designed to address a situation that may cause fear in a horse, particularly if it is in a less-controlled environment out on a trail ride.

We know, rationally, that the water box is to help prepare the person and the horse for when they come to a stream in the mountains or a body of water that will require the horse to walk through it. The ground will be a little softer, and if the horse has never had the experience, never felt that change, it will be really scared at a time when the rider might have less control.

So when the rider starts to ask the horse to walk in the water box, the horse will probably walk up to it but may not step right in. This is where all that horsemanship learning kicks in. Little episodes of cue-pressure-response-release build on each try by the horse. The horse is rewarded with a pet and a verbal "good girl" or "good boy" to provide it with confidence. Together, the veteran and the horse keep taking one small step at a time until the water box becomes more of a curiosity than a threat.

As the veterans work together with their horses to overcome fear and accomplish more complicated tasks, they are also able to see the holes in their human relationships and make plans to navigate through them softly—together.

Finding a Herd

Ultimately, the **HEART OF HORSEMANSHIP**© program is not only about having a relationship with one horse. It's about the brotherhood and sisterhood of the group.

These veterans find a place where they can start to feel trust. But they also get a sense of belonging. They feel like they've found their herd—both with the other veterans and with the horses.

You can't force a group of people to build a bond. But as the veterans go through the program, they become more open. They learn about connection together, and that becomes part of the shared experience. Many relate it to the experience of depending on their brothers and sisters in the combat field, trusting that they have good leadership and knowing that they cover each other's backs.

That's something that we never could factor into the research. I'll let Becky, one of the counselors in our program, explain the benefits of that bond in her own words.

Becky's Story

I wrote a thesis for one of my master's degrees, and the conclusion centered on a study that looked at nurses and their stress levels working in hospitals.

This study was also an eight-week program, and the researchers checked in with the nurses at the beginning, middle, and end of the study, and then followed up after. Even after the program finished, these nurses liked the experience so much that they kept coming together as a group on their own. What the study indicated was that the real stress reduction came from the support they got from each other and the connection they built.

And that's exactly what the veterans experienced with this group. The horses are amazing, but you then add the amazingness of finding your group—plus the

*amazingness of Ellen and Ray and Tom and everybody,
and what we all bring to this group—and it feels like
magic.*

Write It Out

In this journal activity, the veterans are asked to respond to
a series of questions.

What would you describe as your feelings regarding
your sense of purpose?

Has it changed since starting this journey?

Do you feel stronger and more focused on the direction you are going?

Do you let others know your plans so they can guide
and support you along the path?

How have the horses helped along the way?

At this point in the program, the veterans realize how
much the relationship with their horses has progressed. They
are also realizing that it's the second-to-last week—and they
don't want the program to be over yet!

When the veterans started this program, they didn't
know what their response was going to be. But now, some
participants think about how they want to continue riding.
Some think about how much they have left to learn. But

mostly, they just take a little extra time before the last week to really feel that connection from the heart.

And that's where we go next. It was always our goal to find that place where you can live with the feeling of a full heart. The last session is the real recognition of the heart connection—to your horse, or to anyone else in life. Chapter 9 is about how to live with a full heart.

Chapter 9

Feeling Wholehearted

John's Story

In October 2017, a retired Navy SEAL named John showed up in the **HEART OF HORSEMANSHIP**© program. Here are his words to describe how he ended up in our program and what he has gotten from it.

I spent twenty years in service to our country, and I had what I thought was a very successful re-entry into civilian life. The problem was that, at the time, we didn't really speak about things like PTSD. When we did, the SEALs had a mantra: we don't get PTSD—we give PTSD!

So I attempted to button everything up and move forward with my life. But then my life was hit by a truck—literally.

I had PTSD, a traumatic brain injury, and, after the accident, chronic pain. It was a recipe for disaster. I was incorrectly prescribed some medication, so I overdosed and had a psychotic break. I went missing in L.A. and was found foraging in people's backyards, which ultimately led to my arrest.

The VA didn't know what to do with me. I was essentially left to fend for myself. So two weeks after I was released from jail, I ended up at Ellen's ranch.

When I showed up, I didn't know what to expect. I was terrified of interacting with people. But I was in a haze of dullness too. I think I was in shock. I was dealing with all of this intense trauma, and I hadn't experienced people seeing me as a human being for a while.

The first day, we sat in the circle. I didn't know these people, and I didn't trust them, so I didn't feel safe. I was on edge and defensive. All I could think was, Please don't look at me like I'm crazy—I'm not crazy!

But as we went through the rituals in that circle, I started to feel an overwhelming sense of well-being. I experienced energy and a feeling of balance.

When I went to be with a horse in that first session, the horse mirrored me. I was hesitant with it, and it was kind of hesitant with me. Ray, one of the cowboys, asked me, "How is that showing up in your life?"

I said, "I'm terrified of people. I'm terrified of myself. And I don't know what to do about it."

By the end of the session, Reggie—the horse I worked with and that I still work with—had allowed me to be *near him, to touch him and groom him, and I could see that he liked it.*

It was incredibly encouraging to have another living creature allow me to be near it, with no judgment, no preconceived notions, no thinking I was crazy for how I looked or acted. Reggie completely accepted me right there in that moment, and it was incredible.

It took me the entire eight weeks to really process that first moment.

Ellen and the cowboys saw me as human. They saw me as trustworthy. That was important in allowing me to reconnect with the part of myself that they saw—and that Reggie and the other horses saw. As I experienced that acceptance, it became the touch point that fed my healing and kept me coming back.

Celebration and Reflection

When we get to the last session of the program, we ask the veterans to reflect back on where they were at the very first session. Back then, they didn't understand energy, they didn't realize what could happen with a relationship with a horse, and they weren't aware they could feel this kindred spirit.

"What's one of the biggest things that you're taking away from this program?" we ask them.

They tell us how much more confident they are, how

much safer they feel if they go out in a crowd situation. They describe how much less anxious they are, how much the program has improved their relationships with their significant others and their families. They're more aware. They feel more empowered to move forward.

We've had people write comments like this:

"I'm not the diagnosis. I'm still me."

"I can be a productive member of society."

And "I *do* make a difference: this horse appreciates me, and this team of people appreciates me."

We've never had anybody say, "Well, I don't notice any difference."

The hard work—physical, mental, and spiritual—needs to be honored and celebrated as the program comes to a close. We have learned as a team, worked to build partnership, increased our communication skills, improved our self-esteem and confidence, and dared to open our hearts again—all with the help of our equine partners.

Healing Hearts

In full disclosure, I experience a form of PTSD.

My husband Carsten died suddenly several years ago while we were on a vacation to visit the Rock & Roll Hall of Fame. He was misdiagnosed and died as a result of poor standard of care by the doctors and staff at the Cleveland Clinic.

After Carsten died, it was hard for me to do equine therapy with others. Part of my role is to serve as a safety support for the horse and the participant, which means just being there in neutral observation, not making an energetic connection during the session. But each of my horses has its own approach to healing grief. Any time I tried to do therapy sessions, they worked on me and not the client. Because of all the pain I was experiencing, I couldn't go to neutral. I could not really help others for a few years.

It wasn't until we started the **HEART OF HORSEMANSHIP**© program that I again discovered that my horses and I were able to serve others who needed support and healing.

My horses' hearts are open to other people, to serve them during their pain, grief, and suffering. In a sense, animals are Buddhas in themselves, able to recognize suffering and help guide people to a place where grief, trauma, depression, and anxiety can't dominate their life. I noticed the horses were particularly drawn to the work with combat veterans.

Through helping other people, I witnessed myself—along with all those who assisted with the veterans—becoming more mindful of relationships in life and how significant an open heart can be in feeling fully alive.

Building on a Foundation

The eight weeks of the **HEART OF HORSEMANSHIP**© program set up a foundation for healing. But after that initial program, many people want to keep building on that foundation. They want to touch back to the lessons they have learned and the bond they formed.

We do a follow-up one to two months after the end of the program. And that's where we've learned how much of a dosage effect the horses have.

It may not look as big when we reflect on each day's progress, or even from week to week. That may just look like some small steps taken each time. But when we take a step back and look from where each veteran has started to where he or she is now, it's a huge transformation.

The more the veterans ride, the more their autonomic nervous systems stay balanced. When we measure HRV at the follow-up meeting, the effects are still positive. I don't know what other things the veterans have done—maybe they've started to practice meditation or other types of therapies—but the balance is still there. And if the veterans can get themselves into that balanced state, then when they get anxious, they can think about the horse to help them find a sense of ease—and they can activate that physiologically, not just mentally.

Even when we've done the PANAS eight and ten weeks later, it is still really positive: participants show significant improvement from the very first session.

The veterans say they still think about their horse and feel connected even though they don't see it. Most of them say, "I wish we could still ride!" or, "I'd love to come back to the ranch and see my horse!"

The program participants report sustained improvements. Their anxiety has gone down, while their decision-making, focus, and ability to concentrate have improved. If they do go to a dark place, they are able to think of their horse and feel some lightness. *As this book is being edited, we have continued to open the ranch to the veterans who participated in the eight-week program to come out to ride. We haven't conducted official research on them, but the fact that they have shown up week after week for almost a year is a testimony to the healing. A strong bond has formed between them and their horses and the support of the group.*

How to Find Your Herd

You may not be in Southern California, where I am, but you may have accredited therapeutic riding centers near you that can accommodate veterans. I encourage you to find your herd.

People look for certain qualities when they go to a program like this. Some places will just teach you a few techniques and then let you ride horses. But with a heartfelt connection, these qualities—trust, connection, and leadership—become natural outcomes of the program.

As you consider other programs, look for the following.

1. People who truly care
2. A place that isn't trying to make money off of you or exploit your issues
3. A place where you feel safe
4. An accredited riding center/certified therapeutic horsemanship program
5. A program specifically for veterans

Debbie Anderson runs a really successful therapeutic riding program in Indianapolis called Strides to Success, which you can find at http://stridestosuccess.org/. They treat all kinds of people—including veterans. She's also worked with school groups, kids with autism, and survivors of domestic abuse. And we have similar philosophies about showing up with your heart.

Strides to Success

Debbie and her staff can refer you to other people who may have programs in your area.

Hope for Heroes

Debbi Fisher in Seattle runs a veterans program called Hope 4 Heroes (http://www.hope4heroesconsulting.org/). Her program isn't exactly the same as mine, but she has been doing this work for veterans for a long time, is world recognized, and has excellent horses—and she loves working with veterans.

PATH

Debbi is also a consultant to those who want to build programs to work with veterans and horses. She has been on committees of PATH Intl. (Professional Association of Therapeutic Horsemanship International) looking at veterans, so she knows of many other facilities and can refer you as well.

Open Your Heart

As this book comes to a close, you may now have a different sense of an animal as a sentient being to *be* with, rather than just to look at. And you are most likely more aware of the sentient nature, not just of horses, but of all of nature itself.

The power of healing can come from many different directions, but what horses can offer this world is powerful. Their capacity to offer wholeness and love is incredible! We can set up the environment, but the horses are the ones that give you that space to transform. They are not tools; they're partners. And you can learn a lot from a horse.

You just have to know how to listen. And giving the horses more of a voice can help all of us become less judgmental about other people and ourselves. Your partnership with a horse can give you so much more confidence to go out in the world and sustain yourself in a capacity that is not fearful but openhearted.

Not everybody has horses—and not everybody loves horses. So if this isn't your passion, or if it doesn't turn into a passion for finding a journey to your own heart and soul, then you shouldn't do it. But that doesn't mean you can't find passion. It may just reside in a different environment. Find a passion in what you do, whether that's yoga or dancing, walking along the beach, or sailing. Find something that opens your heart.

Wherever you have that connection, you are going to feel yourself open up and expand. So find whatever it is that makes you feel safe again, allows you to build relationships, and moves you to open your heart.

You deserve to be in the world with an open heart full of joy, love, and connection.

ABOUT THE AUTHOR

Dr. Ellen Kaye Gehrke is the founder/director of the **HEART OF HORSEMANSHIP**© program for veterans at Rolling Horse Ranch. She has a Ph.D. from The George Washington University, an MBA from National University and a BSc from the University of California Berkley in Wildlife Biology and Natural Resource Management. She lived and worked in Montana with ranchers and farmers to minimize impact of coal mining and mineral development on ranching and farming. Prior to that she was a team member to plan and implement the backcountry management plan for Yosemite National Park. She was also a recipient of an NSF grant to research Black Bears in Yosemite. She has served as a Dean of Continuing Education, worked in Washington, DC for the National Red Cross and the Department of Agriculture and as a consultant to Booz, Allen, Hamilton. Through the University of Maryland, Dr. Kaye Gehrke spent eight years in Europe teaching and consulting with the US Forces, living in Berlin, Nurnberg, Munich and later in Brussels consulting to an international management education firm.

She has been a professor of leadership, strategy for over 30 years and the last 12 years in Healthcare leadership.

When she and her husband, Carsten moved to the US from Europe in 1996 she finally realized her dreams of owning and working with horses. While adopting a wild horse she realized lessons learned training and communicating with horses and started bringing her leadership classes to the ranch for workshops and seminars. This led to many workshops over the years and the subsequent research that is the foundation for the **HEART OF HORSEMANSHIP**© program.

She is currently a Professor of Leadership and Integrative Health in the School of Health and Human Services at National University in San Diego, California. She has conducted research for more than fourteen years on the human-animal bond, resulting in various publications providing evidence that working and connecting with horses helps relieve symptoms associated with PTSD, stress, and anxiety and improves health and well-being. Since 2005, Dr. Gehrke has been leading equine-partnered workshops for healthcare providers, corporations, universities, non-profit teams, and children at risk. She realized the life lessons horses could teach when she was given Franklin, her first horse, when riding with her mentor/rancher friend in Montana. Later, after adopting an eight-year-old wild mustang, Tonopah, her own journey towards compassion, awareness, and wholeness manifested a desire to help others recognize the healing power of horses. She lives on a small ranch in Ramona, California.

Made in the USA
San Bernardino, CA
22 August 2019